Hope for the Heart
lessons learned in the storms of grief

Robbie L. Casten

XULON PRESS

Copyright © 2011 by Robbie L. Casten

Hope for the Heart
lessons learned in the storms of grief
by Robbie L. Casten

Printed in the United States of America

ISBN 9781613795521

Unless otherwise indicated, Bible quotations are taken from The American Standard Version of the Bible.

www.xulonpress.com

For Gary

Though our time together on this earth was far too brief,

your impact on my life is forever.

Thank you for the inspiration to share a bit of our story.

I believe it is part of "the reason."

CONTENTS

Prologue

If you are reading this, it is probably because you have experienced the death of a loved one. I wish with all of my heart that was **not** the case because I know firsthand that death can leave a soul ravaged and forever changed.

My husband Gary's story, like so many others, had the "c" word involved—bladder cancer. I still remember the doctor asking how many years he had smoked, and being shocked when the answer was "never." And then, when he saw both of us turn pale, how he tried to downplay it with phrases that make me mad to think of now; phrases along the lines of—bladder cancer is very treatable, we caught it early, it really is just a nuisance cancer.

My life changed forever on June 18, 2009 when Gary drew his final breath on earth and began his eternity in heaven, cancer free, care free, worry free, rewarded for the way he lived his life, loved his family and served God. That thought is comforting, but his death and absence in my life have rocked me deeply. I am stumbling through not only the daily changes that I face as a widow and single mom, but the deep emotional, mental, and spiritual impacts of this unwelcome reality.

I am of the opinion that everyone has a story, a book deep within them, that if written would appeal to some and repulse others. My story, from an early age, has been about trying to honor God. Too many times, I have failed in getting that right, but there's this thing called grace that God just keeps extending to me and anyone who asks for it. My story since June 18, 2009 has been about surviving the death of my rock, my love, my best friend, my husband. I'm not an expert on how to make it through grief, but I am experiencing a new depth of God's grace within the storms of grief.

The writings in this book have come about as part of my grieving process. Many are inspired by thoughts that came after attending a grief support program through my church, Willow Creek Community Church in South Barrington, Illinois. Some are my attempt at capturing memories of and honoring Gary—his personality, his huge heart, his "others first" lifestyle. These writings are raw, emotional, deeply personal, and yet I feel compelled to make them available to others.

I hope by sharing my first year lessons, it might show God to you in a new way, just as this chapter of my life has shown me who God is during times of heartbreak so deep that it takes one's breath away. I hope that you will relate at some level, and be inspired to keep putting one foot in front of the other as you weather your storm, instead of curling up into a fetal position like I so often was tempted to do; that you will find comfort in knowing there is a God who sees you, hears you, loves you, and has a plan for you, even in this, your darkest moment.

My prayer is that within these pages, but more importantly, within God's never ending grace, you will find....hope for your heart.

Chaos

Are you a visual learner? Someone who can grasp a concept or new task if you see it performed first? God gave me a visual lesson today.

It was 7:30 a.m. DRAT! Why didn't my 7:00 alarm go off? I remembered to change the hour from six to seven because of my daughter's Friday late day schedule, but I forgot to set the buzzer. DUH! As it turned out, large, loud, road repair equipment outside our house served as my alarm instead. They are ripping up the streets around my community and our cul-de-sac had the privilege of kicking it all off this morning. I watched the progress from my upper bedroom window.

What a process! A big white thing-a-ma-bob (that's the technical term) inched its way around the curb and ripped up the old street. Large concrete chunks flew out a long, overhead shoot and into the back of a semi that was at just the right spot to catch the flying pieces and haul them away. Finally, there were two tractors scurrying around with big brushes and scoops to sweep up the smaller pieces. There were roars and whistles, beeps and buzzers. What a mess! But, when the new pavement gets poured and time passes, we are going to have great streets—smooth and new.

Here's the kicker. There had to be chaos first.

Had any chaos in your life lately? I have. The chaos of cancer and the loss of my husband Gary have made my life a lot like the condition of my street at this very moment. Exposed, unsafe, rough, ugly, unpredictable. But I was reminded this morning that in my chaos, I must keep holding on to what I have believed all my life. God has a plan and can bring good out of chaos.

ripped up roads or dreams
bumpy streets or careers
dead ends or deaths in the family
uncertain routes or medical tests
messy paths or relationships

Order can be restored. I can't get to the order without going through the chaos.

I am eager for this season of chaos to end (or at least subside) but until then, I'm learning to live in chaos because I believe God has a plan.

-odc

Lost Dreams

I t is Tuesday. It's my day to recuperate from Monday. That fact interprets into my most comfortable sweats (the ones that make me an immediate candidate for the "What Not to Wear" cable TV show) no makeup, and a Dunkin Donuts bagel and coffee breakfast. Tuesdays are definitely "recoup" days.

You see, Mondays have become awful ....and wonderful. I'm attending grief support sessions through my church every Monday night. I love the fact that my church has a heart for people who are hurting. As I sit in the parking lot, trying to calm my racing heart and work up enough courage to open my car door and take one step toward facing my loss yet again, I watch others who are also taking brave steps. Steps to work through divorce, addictions, domestic abuse, family relational breakdowns, death, financial distress, stalled careers and a myriad of other life events that leave one reeling.

The faces are like mine—weary, tired, distracted.

The thoughts are like mine— Is this worth it? Does God even care? Am I going to make it through this issue? Am I going to make it through tonight?

The souls are like mine—wounded, anxious, hungry.

Somehow, we all find the strength (guts) to drive onto the church campus, get out of our cars, walk into our assigned rooms, and participate in what we hope will move us closer to being whole again.

Last night's topic in grief support was Grieving the Dream. Pretty self explanatory to those going through it, but maybe not so obvious to those who aren't. When you lose a loved one, you not only lose the person, you lose the future with that person—the goals, the plans, the experiences, the dreams.

I tried to stay distracted all day because I knew this session topic was going to be especially tough. I sit with a group of other people who, like me, had to say good bye way too early to the love of their life. We are a community of sorrow. I knew the topic would wipe us all out, but the session was only two hours long and then it would be over. Or so I thought.

The speaker gave us an assignment. We were instructed to write out the category of our losses at the top of an index card, like: family life, parenting experience, marital relationship, our own health, financial security, community, and then write two or three sentences that specifically reflect that loss. It was tough, and I only made it through one card (and 10 tissues). And then she said the unthinkable. She said we should take the time to complete all our cards and then (here's the kicker) ***make an appointment with grief.*** That's right....actually schedule 15 – 20 minutes several days a week and read through the cards to ***deeply*** experience the feelings

What? Are you kidding? You mean stand exposed and open to this tidal wave of grief that I've been fighting since the day the doctor used the word "cancer?" That's ***exactly*** what she meant. So after my knee-jerk reaction that my losses were way too deep and numerous to do this appointment thing, I've decided to give it a go, because it dawned on me. When it comes to grieving my lost dreams, I can't walk around it. I've got to walk through it and God knows the depth of my pain.

Psalm 139: 1 - 4 (making it personal)
"O Lord, you have searched me and known me. You know when I sit down (to eat alone) and when I rise up (to face another day without my best friend); You understand my (anxious) thoughts from afar. You scrutinize my path (to face my tasks without his encouraging words) and my lying down (in what once was our room in a too empty bed), and are intimately acquainted with all my (sorrow filled) ways. Even before there is a word on my tongue (or a thought of despair), behold, O Lord, you know it all."

So here I go. Where's my tissue box?

- odc

Fog Lessons

Last night in my grief support session, we tackled the question – Where is God in my Grief? (Not a recommended topic for the shallow thinker). We were given six "anchors" to work through this question.

1. This world is broken.
2. Trouble is a part of this life.
3. God moves toward us in our pain.
4. God welcomes our questions and our feelings.
5. God can bring some good out of a difficult situation.
6. God can be trusted.

Really good stuff, huh? But it was a quote from one of my favorite authors, Philip Yancey that really caught my heart. He said, "Life with God may include...times of unusual closeness, when every prayer is answered in an obvious way and God seems intimate and caring. And we may also experience 'fog times,' when

God stays silent, when nothing works according to formula and all the Bible's promises seem glaringly false. Fidelity involves learning to trust that, out beyond the perimeter of the fog, God still reigns and has not abandoned us, no matter how it may appear."

My soon to be sixteen year old daughter is learning to drive a car. Thanks to my husband, who loved all things motorized, he blessed her with a dirt bike at age ten and a four wheeler soon after. Her ever empowering daddy geared her up, showed her a few pointers ("Here's the gas, here's the brake.") and beamed with pride as she zoomed away. They definitely shared the "need for speed."

Because she started early, she had a jump start on the whole driving experience. She got her drivers permit in April and I kept telling my bed- bound husband that he needed to get better and stronger so he could teach her to drive a car because if I had to do it, my daughter and I might kill each other. (I was only half joking.)

Illinois law recently increased the number of months a teen-ager must have their permit, and the number of behind the wheel hours before they test for their license. The new requirements give parents more opportunities to expose their kids to more weather and road conditions and driving situations. (I won't even comment on the rush we parents get from being in a situation where our teens HAVE to admit we are needed in their life. OOPS, too late.)

So, we were coming home the other night and my daughter was driving. When we reached the road that leads to our neighborhood, the trees on each side had trapped in a dense fog. Since this was her first fog experience I went into "instructor mode" and started giving her advice.

"OK, go slower because your range of vision is shortened."

"Use the edge of the road as your guide to where you are."

"There are always deer on this road, so the fog would make it even harder to see them tonight."

"Don't overdrive your headlights."

We were a great team that night. My thirty plus years of driving experience, and her willingness to listen and act on my advice got us home safely. "Great jobs" and high fives all around.

The past four months since Gary lost his battle with cancer are very accurately described as foggy. I would say it has been the fog of the pea soup variety. This season of grief definitely falls into Yancey's "nothing works according to formula" category. What served me well in times of peace and clear vision had to shift when I was driven unexpectedly into the fog of cancer and great loss. So here's what I think God's fog advice is for me.

"Go slow. Your range of vision is obscured with the shadow of death."

"Use the resources I've placed before and beside you to keep moving forward."

"There are still beautiful things to experience in life, but the fog has to clear before they will seem beautiful to you again."

"Don't overdrive your headlights. What's ahead is uncertain, but I can shed light on the next step you take because I'm just beyond where you can't see."

With God's vast wisdom, and my willingness to listen and heed His advice, I can make it home safely, even in the fog times.

High fives all around.

-odc

Foggy Road by Julie D. Ross

Mud Mission

It is our Midwest fall tradition. My family and two other families meet at a local pumpkin farm for a time of hay rides, corn mazes, kettle corn, cider donuts and picking the perfect pumpkins out in the fields. We started the tradition about 11 years ago.

The family structures have changed over the years. We have celebrated new lives and mourned the losses of two. On the surface, we talk about parenthood, the Bears, the economy and our commonalities, but directly beneath the surface stuff is the deeper relationship that comes from years of shared life events—health issues, funerals, new babies, aging parents, job losses, new jobs, battles fought and races well ran.

I always look forward to the pumpkin farm event. It takes me back to my country girl roots and it is usually the last outside event before the weather sends me into hibernation. The big attraction for me at the farm is to watch the pumpkin cannon which can launch huge pumpkins as far as the eye can see. It reminds me of the potato cannons Gary used to build, which were powered by (of all things), hair spray.

This year was tough. It was the first trip to the pumpkin farm without him, and to be honest, both my daughter and I considered skipping the tradition all together. But we made the plans and resisted the easier (but far less fun) option of purchasing our pumpkins at the local Jewel.

Leading up to our planned date, it rained for three days straight. The weather so accurately reflected my soul that week—sad, cloudy, dreary. The "why?" question kept rattling my brain, my peace, my faith.

Our date with the pumpkins arrived and we were blessed with no rain and warmer than forecasted weather. What I think I remember as the sun even showed itself once in awhile from behind the lingering clouds. The fall colors were amazing. God truly orchestrated just the right combination of cool nights, sunlight, rain, and loss of chlorophyll to produce fall colors raised to the tenth power in the northern IL region this year.

When it was time to hit the pumpkin fields, we loaded up on one of the two long flatbed trailers that were pulled behind a huge tractor. Because it had rained so much, the paths into the fields were pure mud and there were even small ponds of standing water in the low lying areas of the fields. With two trailers full of families, hay bales and many pumpkins, we could have easily bogged down in the mud and gotten stuck. Not only would there have been some disappointed perfect pumpkin seekers, but the mess of wading through muddy water to get back to dry ground would have been far from the desired outcome. I am happy to report we didn't sink because our huge tractor had the power to pull the two trailers and their weight loads through the mud and muck of the fields. We made it back to higher ground with our prized pumpkins in tow.

Grief feels a lot like mud. It's not pretty. It can suck you in and slow you down and mess you up—big time. Last night's topic in grief support was "Why, God?" Now this might be a surprise to some, but it is OK to ask that question. I know because I've asked it in various forms—quietly, tearfully, and I've even shouted it a few times—and so far, lots of rain, but no lightning bolts.

I may never know the whys of Gary's way too early end of life on earth (and really, even if I did, would it lessen the impact even one iota?) but here's what I do know. I don't want to get bogged down in the mucky, muddy, mind frame that life will not be good again. It would be very easy for that to happen because Gary had a way of making everything better for everyone around him. Life will definitely never be the same without him, but my prayer is that God (who is my power source) will pull me through the mud and muck of grief that weighs me down in so many ways.

I'm not in that high and dry place yet. Not sure when I'll get there. Not sure in what paths God will lead me to get there. Maybe there will be even more mud to get through. My mud management skills are still far from perfect, but I'm getting better. Lord, I could use a little dry spell.

Psalm 71: 19 & 20 (making it personal)

"For Your righteousness, O God, reaches to the heavens, You who have done great things; O God, who is like you? You who have shown me many troubles and distresses will revive me again, and will bring me up again from the depths of the earth (and the mud and muck of my grief)."

-odc

Hope

I hated high school—except for choir. You see, I was the skinny "goody-goody" girl who didn't fit in with any of the groups that were in our high school. I wasn't a jock (sporty), a freak (dealing with life via questionable substances) or a nerd (all intelligence/no common sense). But high school choir was another story. I not only fit in during choir, I was a leader. My music teacher was awesome. I loved how she exposed us to all types of musical concepts (we once performed an entire Latin mass at a local Catholic church) and how she entrusted me to take a group of my peers off to another piano and help them learn their parts.

As much as I would have loved to love high school (there were some great times) my goal was really to just get through it and get on to college. In other words, do what you HAVE to do, to do what you WANT to do.

My hope was that college would be a better experience for me. I hoped that by choosing a private Christian college there would be more kids who would accept my faith as normal and not weird. I hoped that by pursuing a field of study of my own choosing that I would enjoy the learning process more. I hoped by living on campus amongst so many people of my age, that loneliness from living in the country would end.

When I got to college, I had new hopes. I hoped I could make it across campus to my fourth floor, 7:30AM classes. I hoped that I would click with my roommate; I hoped that I could get a Resident Assistant job so I could afford to stay at my college. And then came a very big hope. I hoped that tall, dark, handsome guy at the foosball table would notice me and maybe ask me out. I heard he was from Chicago. Maybe that hope was pushing it—I mean, really. How often does the country girl/city boy thing work out? College ended up being a great time in my life. So many of my hopes became realities.

Last night in grief support the topic was, "Where is our Hope?" When you experience the death of a loved one, you can feel like all hope is gone, even when you've believed God gives hope all your life.

I held on to the hope that Gary was going to beat cancer until the very last day of his life. Even when the doctors said there was nothing more they could do and sent us home with hospice care my thought was—OK, we're stopping chemotherapy. That's what was making him so sick. Now he's going to get stronger and beat this. That hope was really my prayer.

I would think this every second while caring for him and then (borrowing a term from my good Catholic friends) I would think "Lord, hear our prayer."

For reasons I don't understand, that hope did not become a reality. And the hopes/dreams we had for our future have been filed in the "unfulfilled" category. (Picture an old metal file cabinet. The drawer has been jerked open, the file has been thrown in, the drawer has been slammed several times, the key has been used to lock the drawer and then thrown as far as possible and then the cabinet has been kicked a few times for good measure. That's what I mean by the nice, neat verb—"filed.") I am grieving and will, to some extent, grieve forever our unrealized dreams, our dashed hopes.

But even these heartbreaking, unfulfilled hopes do not shake the *ultimate* hope that my faith gives me. I will see Gary again. Because he lived his life as a forgiven man of God, he has been promised an eternity in heaven and I believe with all my heart, he will be waiting for me there.

I have a dear friend (more like a brother) who coaches his daughter's soccer team. He posted a picture on his Facebook the other day that has inspired me and reminded me of this *ultimate* hope. Before each game, the parents and friends that attend to watch their little soccer players stand in two lines, facing each other. They extend their arms and lean over to touch hands with the person across from them to form what they call a "tunnel of love." The kids run though the tunnel formed by their family and friends, and onto the field. The picture shows the team coming through the tunnel with huge smiles and looks of excitement on their faces. I loved the picture the minute I saw it, and then God gave me this thought.

"That's what heaven is going to be like. All of your loved ones, who loved Me and lived their lives in a way to honor Me, are going to form a tunnel of love for you to pass through as you enter into My presence to see My Son, the One that made eternity in heaven, with Gary, possible for you."

I have had lots of hopes through the years. Some have become realities, others haven't. But I'm learning hope can shape you, motivate you, and keep you moving—even in the worst circumstances.

I grieve with hope.

-odc

Tunnel of Love – Aaron Mayes

Dancing

I attended a very conservative college. I knew going into it there were some pretty strict rules and for the most part, I was OK with living with those rules for the four years I planned to be there. One was **no dancing** (and this was WAY before the bump and grind era. Sing it with me, "Ah, ah, ah, ah, staying alive, staying alive").

In spite of the stance of my college's rule, I always think of joyful events when I think of dancing—times of fun and celebration; homecomings, proms, and weddings. The times when people take extra effort to make themselves look extra special, and celebrate a life event with great joy. Even God's word says, "There is a time for everything and a season for every activity under heaven; a time to be born and a time to die, a time to plant and a time to uproot, a time to weep and time to laugh, a time to mourn and a time to dance." That's right, Pete Seeger only gets credit for the music, the words are from a little older source.

When I was in high school, kids only went to school sponsored dances if they were asked by a date, but today's generation are very "group oriented." If you get asked and want to go with a date, that's OK, but if you don't get asked and want to go, you go with your group of friends. I like this new train of thought. It's much more inclusive.

For the past two years, since my daughter started high school, we have a tradition. Before school even starts, we hit the mall and go homecoming dress shopping. It's a great time. I love watching her try on so many dresses. (It also gives me a small degree of input on the amount of material that needs to be involved). When the perfect dress is found, I can see it in her eyes. The excitement begins that day as we head home with our prize and increases as the day of the big dance draws closer. There is talk of shoes and hairstyles and jewelry and nail polish. I love the fact that my brown belt in karate, 4 wheelin', dirt bike drivin', daughter is also a very "girly girl" when she wants to be.

I haven't felt like dancing lately. That probably qualifies as the understatement of the year. I haven't felt like crawling out of bed lately....but I digress. No desires to dance make sense to me now that I look back at that song from God and Pete. Notice the contrasting verbs?

being born vs. death

planting vs. uprooting

weeping vs. laughing

mourning vs. dancing

I'm mourning huge losses, as are so many people around me lately. It goes against our very nature to want to tango through the tears.

My grief support lesson this week was entitled Joy Will Come Again. Gut reaction when I first read it? Yeah, right! Second reaction? I hope so. A very effective speaker gave us four steps that helped her restore joy in her life after the loss of a loved one. One that caught my attention was what she called praying the Dancing with a Limp prayer. It goes like this.

I am a woman (or a man) who is in grief, but I _____ .

(Fill in the blank with 50 things that bring you joy. No rules, nothing is too big or too small).

I liked it because, as my table group leader pointed out, it's not just "thinking happy thoughts" or going to your "happy place" or any of those other psycho-babble techniques. It is beginning each sentence with acknowledging the loss, the grief, the pain, and then refocusing on something that brings joy. And as I've stated before, I don't want to stay in the pain stage. Gary wouldn't want me to stay there either.

OK...so let's try a few of these.

I'm a woman who is in DEEP grief, but I am blessed with a daughter who is my life and motivation.

I'm a woman who is in DEEP grief, but family and friends are there for me.

I'm a woman who is in DEEP grief, but chocolate can still make me smile. (Nothing too small right?)

I'm a woman who is in DEEP grief, but there will be more days of sunshine on a beach.

I'm a woman who is in DEEP grief, but this cup of McDonald's mocha is warming my hands on this chilly day.

OK, so I'm still not ready to cha cha, and I doubt I would be after placing the period at the end of statement #50, but that's why it's called Dancing with a Limp. To be honest with you, I never was that good of a dancer and dancing takes a lot of lung power so I'm kind of wall-flowering it anyway. But my Dance Instructor is very patient. I just have to be willing to step out onto the dance floor.

Psalm 30:10-12 (making it personal)

Hear, O Lord, and be gracious to me; O Lord, be my helper (as I work through my grief). You turned for me (or someday can turn) my mourning into dancing (with a limp); you loosed my sackcloth and girded me with gladness, that my soul may sing praise (again) to You and not be silent O Lord my God (even when I'm stuck in wallflower mode) I will give thanks to You forever."

-odc

Ornaments

A Not So Jolly Christmas. That's the name of the brochure that was distributed in the last grief support session of this year. They are trying to equip us with anything/everything that might help us through this first year without our loved ones.

So I've done my homework, like the good student that I've always been. I've read lots of grief books and materials and talked to those who are in my same loss situation, trying to prepare and plan for a Christmas I never wanted to face. I'm slowly trying to put a survival plan in action. I'm pretty sure my daughter and I are going to get our sun deprived selves to Myrtle Beach for Christmas week. I'm thinking the roar of the ocean outside my window might be a nice change of pace from the potential blizzard we might be experiencing in northern Illinois, or the tsunami of emotions that might overwhelm me if I stay in familiar surroundings.

Myrtle Beach is where my husband and I honeymooned, so there may be some deep sub-conscious connection there, but I'm telling the truth—it was the only oceanfront spot that was available for Christmas week through our timeshare program. My brother-in-law once made the comment that we acted like we never left Myrtle Beach. He was right. After 26 years of marriage, that's about as good as it can get, huh?

We have a tradition that we started **way back** in 1983 when we got married. We would purchase, or have made, an ornament that represented a major event of that year. So the 1983 ornament has lots of hearts and "Our First Christmas" on it. Some years were pretty low-key and the ornaments celebrate that fact, and some were major events. It's fun to remember each year as we hang them on our tree. Amongst the twenty five, there's one celebrating (the long awaited) Baby's First Christmas, one with Santa on an alligator representing a great vacation, a miniature baby grand representing the real one Gary blessed me with for a wedding anniversary, a silver picture frame with my favorite family picture taken at my daughter's baptism, and then there is last year's.

The beginning of the end started for me on Thanksgiving 2008. Gary and I and my daughter and one of her friends loaded up a rented van and drove to the Orlando area to spend Thanksgiving with Gary's mother. We stayed at a timeshare resort and decided to order our Thanksgiving meal to be eaten poolside. Gary wasn't feeling well, but we thought he had a flu bug, or had eaten something that got to him on the trip down. I noticed he pushed his turkey and potatoes around his plate, just to look like he had enjoyed eating with us, and then we headed back up to the room so he could lie down.

The next day, we had planned a quick trip to Cocoa Beach, FL to get my "ocean fix" and to give my daughter's friend the first time experience of seeing and swimming in the ocean. Gary was too sick to go, but insisted that "his girls" go ahead and he would be fine. We did go, but being at the ocean without him by my side just wasn't the same.

It was just a few weeks after this trip when we got the news that this wasn't a flu bug, and our cancer battles began. When circumstances dictated that he would be spending Christmas in the hospital, we decided to make the best of it. My daughter and I declared it pajama Christmas. If daddy was going to be in pjs, we would be too. We spent the day in a small hospital room, but we were together and pj clad. The 2008 ornament has three pajama clad, night capped family members labeled with our names.

So that brings me to today. It's time to order my 2009 representative ornament. I'm not pondering what the "big event" was. I'm struggling with the temptation to let the tradition die because this one is too hard. That's one of the suggestions to surviving a Not So Jolly Christmas. To re-evaluate traditions.

But this tradition will live on, no matter how difficult it might be, because I know he would want me to keep the memory chain unbroken. This has been a year of hard things, and this will be one more, but I still hear Gary telling me I can do anything I put my mind to. So the tradition will continue. Thanks for the extra strength my love. This year is for you.

-odc

Christmas Perspective

So it's mid December—but you'd never know it by my house. Dear friends came over and pulled out my Christmas tree and decorations boxes and lugged them up the basement stairs, but they are still sitting in the middle of my front room, unopened. I'm contemplating pushing them under the piano and leaving them there until some other dear friends come over and volunteer to take them back down and lift them up onto the high storage shelves from which they came.

I just can't generate the strength (emotional) to open the boxes, put on cheery Christmas music and start decorating this year. The songs, "I'll be Home for Christmas" and "Chestnuts Roasting on an Open Fire" make my heart hurt because he **won't** be home for Christmas and "Chestnuts" was our favorite cuddling song. I accidentally clicked on Celine Dion's version of "Blue Christmas" on YouTube the other day and almost flooded out my desktop before I could "x" out the tab to turn it off. Music has always touched my soul more deeply than any other form of expression.

I have memories of happier Christmases, and those warm my heart a bit. Christmases spent with his side of the family where Gary was always the designated "present distributor." Christmases spent with my side of the family that were filled with lots of great food, laughter and music. Although Gary didn't participate in the music, he was always the one walking around with the coffee pot to fill up cups, or in the kitchen doing dishes so the musicians could carry on. There were Christmas mornings at our own home with our daughter as she graduated from the most desired gift being a Barbie play house to the most desired gift being a Jeep Wrangler. But this Christmas.....words fail me. I was talking with a friend of mine who lost his wife to cancer one month before Gary lost that same battle, and he summed it up well. He just wants to get through Christmas. We're both looking forward to Christmas, but not in the way most people are.

So my life circumstances have changed since last December, but the *real* focus of Christmas, or to put it in that 80's slogan that was so popular, the reason for the season, has not, nor ever will change. It is the birth of Christ. As a matter of fact, this Christmas I'm concentrating on the fact that the birth of Christ means even more to me now, since it was the beginning of the provision of heaven.

I wonder what Christmas in heaven is like. Have you thought about that? Talk about the birthday party to end all birthday parties!

Budget – unlimited.

Decorations – gold, silver, and every precious gem you can name.

Menu – everyone's favorites (and my personal belief that calories are a non-issue).

Music – angelic choirs.

Invitation list – All those who realize Christ is their only Hope and have left the earth.

That means Gary is invited. I'm not – yet. So this first Christmas apart in twenty five years is not what I planned, but I can still celebrate the One who came to earth in the form of a newborn, in order to make Gary's first Christmas in heaven possible.

And so I will, though not in the usual ways. That means sand instead of snow for sure, as we're planning to head toward the east coast Christmas week. And so far it's looking like that also means the Christmas decorations are staying in their boxes this year, but I think that's OK. My daughter and I are still in grief survival mode, and if that means the tree doesn't get put up and the stairwell doesn't glisten with greenery and ribbons, then so be it. As long as we're changing things up a bit, I'm thinking Christmas dinner will be grilled burgers on the beach and birthday cake for dessert, minus the candles, of course.

Happy Birthday Jesus.

-odc

Calendars

It's January, and that means a new calendar. Paper calendars are becoming a bit passé, now that everyone keeps their schedules online, but I still like to hang a calendar with big white squares in my kitchen and write in the day's appointments. People usually pick these wall calendars based on their particular interests. I've seen calendars of all kinds: animals, motorcycles, the Far Side, nature, folk art, sports, favorite locations, swimsuits (ahem) and even my vote for most unusual this year—outhouses.

For the past several years, my calendar has been from Camp Paradise, our church's camp located in the upper peninsula of Michigan. Each month shows amazing pictures of kids and their dads in the deep woods beauty of Michigan. You can almost hear the squeals and laughter as you look at pictures of campers canoeing, swimming, wall climbing, tackling the high ropes course, shooting arrows in the archery area, swinging off rope swings, zip-lining, jumping off the water trampoline, congregating at the campfire under star lit nights, spending rare one-on-one time together in that pure, untouched wilderness. These priceless moments come only when a parent purposefully puts themselves and their children into an environment without the distractions of work, school, cell phones, computers and never ending to-do lists. (Camp is also without running water, electricity and flush toilets and includes wood burning water heaters and bucket showers, which I think is why it is DAD/son and daughter camp instead of MOM/son and daughter camp.)

There is another group of people featured in this calendar. They are the work weeks and camp staff volunteers who spend hours and months of their extremely valuable time each year for the camp to become the memory making paradise it is for every person who rides The Queen (the pontoon boat) up the river to the shores of camp. Thousands of volunteer hours have been spent planning, clearing, building, tearing down, remodeling, concrete pouring, solar panel installing, roofing, painting, menu planning, cooking, cleaning, serving, counseling, life-guarding, music leading, high ropes course facilitating, nursing, program directing and a multitude of other roles that are involved to pull off camps in the months of June, July and August.

Every year, around January 1ˢᵗ, I take down the old year calendar and write in all the birthdays and school day events in the new year calendar. It is always nostalgic to look back at what filled up the year that has just passed. I'm always tempted to not toss the old calendar, but tuck it into a place where I could look back at the events and remember them at some point in the future. Then my anti pack rat tendencies kick in and I say, "Out with the old, in with the new."

This year's calendar transfer process was bittersweet for several reasons. For the first time in many years, my husband's face was missing from that group of men and women who were the camp work week volunteers. He was working on his private battle with cancer this past year, and was unable to be present to contribute his roofing expertise (or I should say roofing perfectionism), muscle, can-do spirit, junk food supplies, and never ending passion for camp and all it stands for.

The other reason it was tough was because in many of those white squares was the word "chemo." It was odd to see the words associated with cancer (chemo, doctor, test, hospital) interspersed with the words of life continuing in spite of Gary's battle (cheer competition, dentist, hair appt., birthday, wedding). It reminded me that in spite of the loss of life, dreams, hopes and security— life continues.

I am now learning to live a different life, an unexpected life, a life no one saw coming. One that no longer includes the man who took a never broken vow to love me unconditionally (and believe me, there are many conditions) and be by my side until God took one of us home.

On June 18 2009, Gary went home. (I'm still thinking it was *way too early* God.) Away from "his girls" who loved him dearly, but also away from hospitals, chemo recliners, oxygen compressors, and the many burdens and blessings that come with life on earth. That date also happens to have been the opening session of 2009 at Camp Paradise. Coincidence? I think not. I like to think Gary took a "fly by" on his way to heaven to do a final inspection on the camp roofs, just to make sure they were all set for another camp season.

I broke my anti pack rat rule this year. I tucked the 2009 Camp Paradise calendar into the bag of other mementos that I've chosen to keep. As I turn the pages of my calendar this year and see the camp pictures, I may not see Gary's picture, but I will see traces of Gary in every smiling face that takes that boat ride to camp and sleeps beneath the roofs that he so lovingly (and he would want me to add—PERFECTLY) worked on. His legacy lives on.

I Corinthians 15:58 (making it personal)

"Therefore, my beloved brethren, (my dear husband), be steadfast, immovable, (thank you that you were) always abounding in the work of the Lord (at Camp Paradise), knowing that your toil is not (nor ever will be) in vain in the Lord."

- odc

Camp Paradise Riverfront – Curtis Vanden Bos

Coffee

G rowing up the fifth child of Southern born and bred parents was a lesson in the fine art of eating and drinking, southern style. That meant lots of pinto bean soup and cornbread. (By the way, true southern cornbread is **not** sweet and is often eaten crumbled into a large cup of cold buttermilk), vegetable soups made mostly from our own, or our neighbors' gardens, green beans and new potatoes cooked for so long they melt in your mouth, summer dinners of fresh sweet corn and thick sliced tomatoes, and the every Sunday meal, pot roast with onions, carrots and potatoes. I woke up every Sunday to the mouth watering aroma of a perfectly seasoned beef roast browning on the stove. It was then covered and left to slowly cook, while we were at church.

Drinking didn't involve what you might think, since we were a teetotaler family, but it did involve coffee—strong and black and lots of it. I don't ever remember seeing an empty coffee pot in our country kitchen. My parents were both big coffee drinkers (all day, every day) and my father was famous for giving all the grand-kids their first taste of coffee via what he called "coffee soakers," a donut or cookie dunked into coffee. Fortunately, the little ones didn't form any caffeine addictions at such a young age, but it never failed to elicit much laughter from all those watching the facial expression of the first time taster.

I didn't really acquire the love of coffee that my parents had, until I experienced the many and varied offerings of Starbucks a few years ago. Put chocolate on anything, and I most likely will love it, so it was mochas that really kick started my coffee crav-ings. I eventually graduated to other flavorings like caramel or cin-namon, and by now have probably tried all of the Starbuck coffee creations.

I miss Starbuck nights. Almost every night on his way home from work in the city, my husband would call me and ask, "Is it a Starbucks night?" And it was such a treat when he would come through the door with a hot cup of the coffee choice of the day. He would hand it to me with a big smile and a kiss. This was so typical of him. His whole life was spent giving, thinking of how he could make someone else's day a little brighter, no matter what kind of day he had experienced.

One night, when mocha was the coffee craving of choice, there was an incident. Just as Gary was turning into our neighborhood, it tumbled out of the cup holder and spilled all over his truck. After a very long day, and a valiant attempt at fulfilling the request, most men would have put a mark in the "I tried" category, said a few choice words, and complained loud and long about the mess clean up that was now required. Not my Gary. His reaction was to look at the clock and determine if he still had enough time to make a mad dash up to our local coffee shop to get a replacement mocha, before it closed. Did I mention that Gary hated coffee and could hardly even stand the smell of it? And now there is one spilled all over his vehicle, which he held in esteem just slightly lower than his family members. And most amazingly, I would have never even known about the spill, except I recognized the cup was from our local shop, not Starbucks, and I asked him about it.

Tonight has been one of those "feeling blue" nights. It's a cold, snowy night in the Chicago area. After dinner, I needed something warm; just to raise my body temperature and my spirits a bit. As I was making a cup of instant coffee (sorry Mom and Dad!) it reminded me of those endearing Starbuck nights, and that night in particular when the mocha took the tumble. It was one of the many times that Gary modeled to me how to love others in creative, simple, meaningful, "others first" ways.

In the last few weeks of Gary's life, I received several phone calls from people I had never met who would say, "I want to tell you a story about what your husband once did for me." Those stories would involve acts of kindness that ranged from someone getting a Casten Roofing umbrella handed to them during a downpour, to how he always had dollar bills tucked up in the visor of his truck so he could easily hand them to the "need work/money" guys standing at the expressway ramps, to Gary shifting work from his own company to somebody who desperately needed a job to get them through a tough financial situation. These stories didn't surprise me, but just like the mocha mission, I would have never known about these acts because Gary was a behind the scenes blesser. His acts of kindness were never done in a way to draw attention to himself. I still have so much to learn from his example.

Between the hot cup of (instant) coffee (which *did not,* for many reasons, compare to my Starbucks treats by any stretch of the imagination) the fleece blanket that has become a part of my around the house winter wardrobe, and the memories of my love and his giant servant and giver's heart, I'm feeling a bit warmer. But more importantly, I'm feeling inspired to be a kinder person, in spite of any life circumstance.

See my love; you are still making me a better person, even in your earthly absence. Not that's what I call a legacy.

Galatians 5: 22 and 23a (making it personal)
(Thank you Gary for so beautifully demonstrating) The fruit of the Spirit is love, joy, peace, patience, kindness, goodness, faithfulness, gentleness and self-control."

-odc

Coffee Message - Susan Listhartke

Triggers

I call them "triggers." They sneak up on me and take me by surprise. I'll be doing just fine and then something happens, or I encounter a situation and boom! I'm a wreck. Sometimes the emotion is deep sadness, sometime it's anger, sometimes it's a long heart-wrenching cry, sometimes it's the defeatist attitude that nothing will ever be good again without him here to work through the major life issues, much less the minor ones like changing the filter in the furnace, or knowing the source of that strange noise coming from my car.

One day it was the smell of his cologne as I opened his closet. Once it was when I accidentally dialed his cell phone number instead of the one just one digit different from his, and I heard his voice mail message. Other days, it's hearing the songs from his final celebration of life service, or finding yet another cup of loose change. Even a TV commercial can do it. It's the one where the mother and father are at their daughter's college and are taking her out for a good meal while they visit. My heart hurts because we won't get to do that together now.

Today, the trigger was a form letter from the village where I live. It started with these words,

"It has recently come to our attention that during the last snow event, as a result of sidewalk or driveway clearing at your home, snow and ice was left in the roadway near your residence. Pushing snow into the roadway is against Village ordinance and you may be cited for this action."

At first I was angry. (I'll be the first to admit that my normally rational thinking becomes a bit "skewed" when the anger thing comes over me). How did they come to the conclusion that there is snow or ice in the roadway by my house? Did a neighbor call and tell them? And if so, that takes some nerve! My neighbors know Gary passed away this summer and I'm unable to clear the snow myself. And for years Gary was the one who went out and removed the snow from *their* driveway and sidewalks after doing ours! It is possible that my car tires carried snow from the driveway as I went in and out, but it's not like we intentionally shoveled the snow into the street!

And so I called the office of the sender of this notice. Probably by an act of God, I got an answering machine and left a message requesting a return call. That gave me time to cool down a bit. Within the hour I received that return call. (Small town living does have its advantages.) I tried to stay calm and asked if he could tell me how he had gotten this information. Was it reported by a neighbor? Of course, he couldn't tell me the source. And then it happened. I went from mad to sad as I tearfully explained that this would be **very disappointing** if that was the case because.....and I told him the whole story, including the fact that my husband used to remove snow from other drives and walkways in our cul-de-sac and all the way down to the bus stop. He listened patiently and sincerely offered his condolences, and advised we just try to make sure it didn't happen again at the next snowfall. I wanted to reiterate that we didn't push snow out into the street, but instead I thanked him for letting me vent and then hung up.....and the floodgates opened.

My tears gained momentum as my mind finally formed the question that I've been trying to force down—Just how am I supposed to do life without him? Snow removal is just the "tip of the iceberg." I threw the question up to God and gave in to a nice long therapeutic cry that increased in intensity when my daughter walked into the room. She wrapped her arms around me and shared my moments of grief. Her shoulder absorbed my tears.

I wish I could say I had a nice neat answer for that question—but I don't. I just know I have to keep putting one foot in front of the other and continue hoping that like all the other trying times in my life, God sees, God hears, God loves, and God has a plan.

Later, after my tears had dried and I had survived the latest trigger episode, I had to smile as I remembered another snow story that took place at a recent family gathering. My brother and his son plow snow in the winters. We were talking about the upcoming snow predictions and the stretches of days without sleep they sometimes endure to get their plowing commitments completed. My brother told an Uncle Junior story.

My Uncle Junior was a man of *strong* opinion, and was never one to hold back giving it, usually with several "colorful expletives" thrown in for emphasis. (I bet most families have their own Uncle Juniors). He had this to say about snow removal (paraphrased a bit for all ages of readers). "I'm not going to go out and move it. I didn't put it there; I'm not getting rid of it." I wonder how my kind village superintendent would have responded to that comment on his form letter.

Triggers. I understand they are a normal part of the grieving process, whatever *normal* is. I'm sure I'll experience them for the rest of my life. The privilege of knowing a love so deep is why I grieve at all. I'd do it all again.

And Uncle Junior, I'm with you. LET IT SNOW!

-odc

Monday

"**M**onday, Monday, can't trust that day." (The Mamas and the Papas.)

I remember hearing this song as a little girl, while my older sister was groovin' to the 60's era music. Fast forward to my teen years in the 70's, and it was the tear jerker lyrics of the Carpenters that I sang along with. "Rainy days and Mondays always get me down." And more recently, Jordin Sparks talks about that fateful first day of the week with her song Permanent Monday. "Cuz every time you go away the sunshine starts to fade, frozen by the hands of time into a permanent Monday."

Let's face it, Mondays tend to get a bum rap, not only in music lyrics, but in the mere thought of another one coming to kick off five (or more) work days before those coveted days off.

About four months ago, Mondays became days of great angst for me. I started attending grief support on Monday nights at my church. I'd sit in my car and gear up the nerve to open the door, get out and walk into the building. Once inside the doors, I'd hit the closest restroom, just so I could still my pounding heart and take deep breaths in order to make it the rest of the way to the class location. (Can you say panic attack?)

That first Monday night was the hardest. As usual, the grief support leaders had done everything to make it as easy as possible. Those working the check in area were efficient and kind. There were greeters at the door to offer guidance or answer questions, and walk with you to find your table, if needed. There were ample supplies of home baked goodies and coffee and teas available. (I hit the chocolate options hard, since it is my personal believe that chocolate is the sixth stage of grief!) My table leader was there to introduce himself and welcome each of us personally. I knew from a friend who had been to these meetings in the past that tables were assigned by "loss type" so everyone at my table (including my leader) was a "spouse loss" person. I think without even knowing that ahead of time, I could have determined that fact because we all shared this "can't believe I'm here, half of me is gone, I'm ready to bolt" look.

During the many difficult events of that kick-off night, I remember two that "took the cake." At one point, we were asked to go around the table and mention the full name of our deceased love one. For me, and I'm sure for probably everyone else too, it was the first time I had said my husband's full name out loud since he lost his battle with cancer. Just saying his name brought back his forever handsome face, his gorgeous brown eyes, the overwhelming sense of love that I had for him and he for me, and the all too familiar ache in my heart caused by his earthly absence. The second activity that even topped that emotional experience was when we were given time to tell our story—how and when we met, number of years married, children, the events leading up to and cause of death. I cried with each story and somehow choked out mine and Gary's story too. That night was exhausting. Our table would have won the "most tissues used" award if there would have been one. Hands down.

Fast forward four months to just this past Monday. I started the second session (another nine weeks) of grief support. I am proud to report that I did **not** have a panic attack as I walked in the main doors of the church. Instead, I felt an overwhelming sense of peace and an assurance that I had done the right (albeit difficult) thing by attending and engaging in those first nine weeks of grief support sessions. And, that I was doing the right thing by returning for the next nine weeks.

We have four returning table members and five new ones. As we heard the new members tell their stories, I once again cried with them, and empathetically recognized the pain that poured from their hearts as they struggled with intense emotions and cracking voices. And the tissue boxes got hit hard once again. But my new "community of sorrow" members don't know what a gift they gave me that first night of their attendance. I realized that I was them, four months ago. And there is some healing going on deep within me. It hasn't come easily, or as fast as I would have liked, and it is *far* from complete. (Not sure that's even possible). But I know for a fact that I have taken some steps away from that heart wrenching agony that I was in just four short, but in some ways, four very long months ago.

In the early days of grief, hope and happiness seem so elusive, so distant, and you wonder if you'll ever make it to those "better" life stages again. They are the Mondays of the grief journey. I think I'm still a long way from Saturday (and I like to think Sunday will be when I join Gary in heaven) but it feels like I might be in the 12:01 AM timeslot of Tuesday now. I'll take it! In an attempt to be optimistic, perhaps I should start singing some Saturday songs.

In honor of my Chicago boy…..."Saturday, in the park, I think it was the 4th of July."

-odc

And

nd versus *or.*

The battle of the conjunctions. I didn't realize this battle was raging in my life, but at grief support, our speaker called me out.

In the pain of grief and loss and serious skepticism that life can ever be good again, we mourners can get a lot of things wrong. We are more likely to have accidents, develop illnesses, and be unable to focus on the task at hand. That sounds like a Grief 101 lesson, but I can attest that these statements are true. In the first two months following my husband's death I (1) blew through a busy intersection red light on the way to his gravesite, (2) was hospitalized for a recurring lung infection and (3) had too many examples of the "lack of focus" statement to fit onto this page.

We heart heavy mourners can make unwise decisions and not use sound judgment on people and situations, in spite of having a good track record on these things prior to the death that pushes us into our new, unwanted reality . Our thoughts can become skewed, especially if we just go by our feelings that day, and not by the more desired equation of

feelings + truth + intellect.

I have always thought myself a clear thinker. A black and white thinker if you please—heavy on the intellect and truth, lighter on the feelings. (Confession – maybe too light on the feelings at times). But now I find myself in quite the opposite thinking pattern. If I had to assign a color to my thinking now, it would definitely be gray. A very dark gray. Maybe charcoal gray. Trying to do life without Gary has forced me into making a concerted effort to keep that feelings part of the equation from getting more than its fair share. When that happens, truth and intellect get cheated. Here are a few thoughts that are examples of this unbalanced thinking:

I can be angry at God or I can love Him, but not both.
I can be sad or I can believe life is good, but not at the same time.
If God allowed my loved one's death to happen, then I can't trust Him anymore.
I'm in such pain; I won't ever feel joy again.

I've had these thoughts. Other members at my grief support table admitted they have too. It was good to know I wasn't alone in this dark thinking, but I needed to hear some thoughts on how to get *out* of that pattern because to be honest, it's not helpful, it's exhausting, and it's not how I want to think for the rest of my life. Our speaker threw out a lifeline when she challenged us to drop the *or*, and embrace the *and*. So the unbalanced thoughts reworded would say:

Can I be angry at God *and* still love Him?
Can I be so, so sad *and* still believe life is good?
Could God have allowed this to happen *and* still be worthy of my trust?
Can I be in such excruciating pain *and* still feel joy, even laugh sometimes?

OK, that works. It still allows me to express the feelings, because those are still intense and raw and need to be expressed, but it also adds in that intellect factor, and there are lots of Truths (with a capital "T") in God's word that tell me that there is a "yes" answer for each of these questions. Friends that are a few steps farther down the grief road than me assure me that they are finding a yes answer to those questions too. To hear that gives me the strength I need to keep going.

One little word shift (*and* for *or*) a balanced thought equation, and the hope that the grays get a little lighter with time. Dare I hope for Technicolor?

- odc

Still Celebrating

H ere it comes. Another first. This one will be hard because of
who he was.

He was a hopeless romantic, a man who showed his affection
many days in many ways, but Valentine's Day is when he pulled
out all the stops. Sometimes there were big events, sometimes
there were small reminders, but every demonstration of his love
made me stop and thank God for the many miracles He worked
in order for this man to choose me, with whom to spend his short
life.

One of the big events when we were dating was when he
had arranged a special evening, but wouldn't tell me any other
details. He just advised that I "dress up." Having recently learned
of my great love for live theater, he had arranged for us to see
"My Fair Lady" (he said it was a foreshadowing title) with Rex
Harrison at the Arie Crown Theater in Chicago. Now that in and
of itself would have been enough to impress this country girl, but
when he bypassed all of the traffic to the general parking and gave

his name to the security guard, we were directed to a coned off parking space approximately ten feet from a private door. Upon presenting our tickets, we were ushered up to a private balcony that seated about ten people. I was blown away that night by his thoughtfulness (and his Chicago connections – thank you Uncle Harold) that enabled us to enjoy such a beautiful, meaningful evening at the theater. Most of Gary's greatest joy in life came from bringing joy to other's lives.

It was just the start of a love story that endured for twenty six years, not perfect because of the imperfect parties involved, and like everyone, we had our fair share of tough life events—but throughout it all, he often reminded me he was here to stay. Flowers and Fannie May and secret messages, door to door deliveries and opening doors and helping me with my coat, beautiful jewelry (he had our local jewelry store in his speed dial numbers) pumping my gas and washing my car, installing an automatic car starter so it would be warm on the days he wasn't here to do it for me. Friends and family members used the word "spoiled" but he always smiled and said, "No, just greatly loved." The truth? Both.

Every February, I would ask him the same question. "Will you be my Valentine this year?" He would make a big production out of the question. He would roll his eyes and sigh heavily and then say, "Well……I guess." And his planning would begin. About one week prior to February 14th, he would hand make an elaborate menu, giving me several options for each course of the dinner he would make for me on Valentines evening. He would leave the menu in an obvious area so I could find it and make my choices, giving him enough time to do the shopping and preparing for his special meal. The evening of Valentine's Day, he transformed our living room into the Casten Café, complete with a candlelit table in front of the fireplace, fine china and ambiance music, and then serve his carefully prepared meal with such pride. (He always joked that he was only doing it for the tip).

So many good memories. A great love so beautifully demonstrated. I am so grateful for having known an earthly love like this because I know that not everyone does. Or, people start down that path and then for many reasons, that path dead ends. It is so easy to fall into the fatalistic thinking that love is over forever when love stories get interrupted or go awry. When the pain of a lost love becomes overwhelming, we are tempted to pull back from ever risking that pain again. We don't agree with the "better to have loved and lost, than never to have loved at all" adage. It might take a lot to convince us that if we had such a great love story once, lightning will strike twice. Or, we wrestle with the more philosophical question—why would lightning strike twice for us when it doesn't strike once for others?

The truth is, we all have a deep, God-given desire to love and be loved, not just on a spiritual level, but on an earthly level too. I think Nat King Cole got it right in his song "Nature Boy" when he sang, "The greatest thing you'll ever learn is just to love, and to be loved in return."

The Casten Café will be closed this Valentine's Day because the owner/operator has left this world. I am convinced that he is now in the presence of the Source of all Love, the One who said, "Well done" to him when he was judged on how well he loved those put into his life. The many years of unconditional love that Gary gave me will never be forgotten and has changed me forever. I aspire to love those God has put into my life (and those to come) the way Gary did. Having known that love, and still feeling it even now, is what I will celebrate this Valentine's day, the first without him.

John 15:17 (making it personal)
(Hey my love, thanks for getting this one so right). "This I command you, that you love one another."

- odc

Words

"If there is anything I've learned, or I'm learning, it's that whatever you're feeling in that moment, it's okay. It's okay, it's okay to feel numb, and for me it's like anger, shock, denial, it's okay. Or just that feeling like you don't feel anything at all, and that's okay too. It's okay to have no answers, and no explanations, and maybe no words."— From Rob Bell's "Matthew"

No words. To be speechless. That hasn't happened a lot in my life. I have "the gift of gab," and to be honest, tend to fill quiet times, when they would have best be left quiet, with words. But recently, when it mattered most, words escaped me. But not him.

I have met several people through grief support sessions that have gone through my same life changing loss. No death is easy, but the death of a spouse seems to cut **extremely** deep. Or perhaps, since it is my loss, it just seems that way. God describes marriage as the "two becoming one," and I was one of the blessed where this was definitely true. When death takes a marriage partner in a "two to one" marriage, the one left feels a devastatingly deep sense of unbalance, incompleteness, and aloneness.

Several of my spouse loss friends were given great gifts during the final days of their loved ones life. Their spouses journaled their thoughts, struggles, memories, words of love. Some wrote birthday cards for the next several years to their children. Some recorded video taped messages so there would be a forever captured image and final words.

When we were given the very grim news that chemotherapy was no longer winning the cancerous battle raging within Gary's body, I wanted to process it in my typical way—with words. I wanted to talk about it. I wanted him to talk about it. I wanted to know what he was feeling and tell him what I was feeling. I wanted him to talk to others and to his spiritual mentors. I wanted him to tell me about his fears, his words of advice for our Chicago based business and how to parent our daughter. I wanted him to reminisce about his childhood, his college years, our courtship and early days of marriage. But in his typical fashion, he didn't say much.

Part of me thinks it was because he thought that by talking about these things, it would mean the doctors were right and he wasn't ready to stop fighting the cancer. He never was a quitter. And I know for a fact that since he lived his life trying to make mine better in every way possible, he knew talking about these things would make me think the battle was over and send me reeling. And, as usual, he was so right. I'm not sure I could have continued to care for his every need with the same feeling of hope that my actions were going to help him get better, if I really knew they were the very last acts of love I would ever perform for him.

So he didn't talk or reminisce or give advice or plan. He stayed silent on these things. But the twenty six years of marriage leading up to this time were crammed full of words: words that were uplifting, encouraging, consoling, challenging and to be honest, careless, (on very rare occasions). Words that included inside jokes, secret messages, I'm sorrys and forgive mes, words of concern and hope, of spiritual things and silly things, of deep thinking and life dreaming. And those words will forever be a part of our "two as one" story.

At the specific moment when the doctor told us there was nothing more that could be done, we both were at a loss for words for awhile. We simply held each other and cried—and then Gary broke the silence. He looked me in the eyes and said, "I love you." Not "I don't believe this" or "there must be a mistake" or "why God?" but "I love you."

In the days between that moment and the one where Gary peacefully slipped into heaven, I honored his decision to not talk excessively because that's who he was all his life—a man of few words. But when he did speak, the words were the most important three that he knew I needed to hear, and would hang on to until we meet again. And that says it all.

-odc

Storms

When I was growing up, we didn't have an excess of money. My parents were Southerners who migrated north to the state of Illinois, and worked hard to provide the basics (and some "luxuries") to me and my four siblings. The beauty of that statement is that I never really felt deprived because love and security can fill up a lot of other gaps in a young life.

In spite of not having an over abundance of money, my parents sacrificed and saved and planned for family vacations. Most years, we would take long road trips back to my parents' roots—the beautiful Smoky Mountains of eastern Tennessee. We would set up camp in the mountains at a campground called Horse Creek. Over the years, our shelters progressed from tents, to a truck shell, to a pop up camper, to a full size trailer, to a fifth wheel trailer, and eventually, to a motor home—due to my parents increased earnings and decreased at home kid count. (Being the youngest has its advantages!)

Horse Creek was not a luxury campground, by any means. There were no shower houses or plumbing of any kind, no camp stores or in ground swimming pools, but it was a luxury campground in our minds due to the pristine beauty of the mountains, the ice cold mountain creek that ran through it, and the ever popular swimming holes where my sisters and I learned that Southern boys learn to flirt at a very young age.

My mom would call and tell our Tennessee "rellies" when we would be arriving so they could come visit us. The time there was filled with family gatherings involving a ridiculous amount of food cooked over the open flame in huge pots and cast iron skillets, hikes through the mountains, music around the campfire, and chasing watermelons down the creek that had slipped out of their rocked in cooling places. Years prior to my being there, the Smokys were the backdrop for my parents' courtship. Little did they realize that someday the voices and laughter of their children and grandchildren would echo through those same mountains.

Several years ago, I remember how saddened I was to hear that when a huge storm had ripped through Tennessee, Horse Creek had been devastated. The beautiful mountain stream where I chased loose watermelons had become a raging river as the torrential rain fed into its strength. As it roared down the mountain and through the camping area, it leveled trees, carried huge boulders down from the upper areas, flooded camp sites and changed the whole geography of our beloved vacation spot. Rebuilding was a must and was going to be very costly. Some doubted it was worth the rebuild effort, but a plan was implemented and today, Horse Creek is still available for hiking and camping. It isn't the same as it was prior to the storm, but it survived.

"Loss changes forever the geography of your soul." That's a quote from my grief support session. Just like my pre-storm memories of Horse Creek, life prior to the ravages of my husband's cancer diagnosis was filled with good times, great memories, beautiful life events heavy on the laughter; but when the storms of illness and death ripped through our home, my soul took some devastating hits and has been forever changed. There is an undeniable need for heart healing and soul rebuilding.

Our speaker suggested a plan.

1) *Time – This is not a sprint; it will be a life long journey.*
   This will be a challenge for me. I've always been a "get it done" kind of gal.
2) *Tasting – There's a scripture that says, "Taste and see that the Lord is good. Blessed is he/she that takes refuge in Him."*
   I am desperate for refuge from this storm, one of the worst I've ever weathered. Based on past life storm survivals, I'm choosing to take refuge in God once again.
3) *Togetherness – When your trust isn't strong on your own, leaning into someone else's is advised and encouraged.*

I have been leaning a lot lately and am grateful God has placed those in my life that are good at "weight-bearing" my heavy heart and scarred soul.

I sure didn't want this storm. It has been far too costly; but as much as I desired and prayed for it to happen, this storm didn't blow off course. It came at me full force. There was no evasion, no choice. I didn't think I would survive this one, and I have told God that many times in the past year and a half, but so far, I have. The geography of my soul is forever changed, but I'm still trusting in my Storm Shelter.

Isaiah 25: 4a
"For You have been a defense for the helpless, a defense for the needy in his distress, a refuge from the storm."

- odc

A Mother's Lament

Three steps forward, one step back. That's how Richard Foster described the dance. "For a thousand years, Christians did a dance called the tripudium to many of their hymns. As worshipers sang, they would lock arms and take three steps forward, one step back, three steps forward, one step back. In doing this, they were actually proclaiming a theology with their feet. They were declaring Christ's victory in an evil world, a victory that moves us forward, but not without setbacks."

I picked up my 16 year old daughter from track practice after school tonight. Her face was flushed bright red from having run several miles during her work out. As usual, she had a friend with her that needed a ride home and had offered that we could be the transport. I didn't mind. It makes me proud that she is noticing others in need and wanting to help them. She's becoming more and more like her dad in that respect.

On our way home from her friend's house, she shared with me how much she was enjoying track and how much less stress she felt since she had upped her physical activity. We talked about something so sacred between a mother and daughter that I won't share it here, but between the two of us, we came up with a plan that fulfilled her request and made me proud and would honor her dad. How much better can that get? I sent up a silent prayer of thanks for what I hoped would be the start of a three step forward time for her. God knows we both needed it.

She requested her usual dinner – pasta, and so I prepared her favorite dish in her favorite style. After eating, she informed me that she was going to hit the shower. I heard her head up the stairs with a few groans from the aching muscles that had been worked extensively at practice and had stiffened as she sat and ate. I heard her bathroom stereo music (did you know teenagers can't take showers without music in the background?) and then the sound of the shower. All was well. Three steps forward. But then I heard it — sobbing. You see, it's in the shower where she lets out all of her emotions; whether they stem from a bad day at school, a careless comment from a peer, the ending of a relation-ship or, more often these days, the sorrow that comes from losing her rock, her security, her "go to" guy – her daddy.

Just like when she was a newborn and I learned to distinguish the meaning of her cries, I am learning to do that all over again. There are varying intensities to her shower cries. Some are rela-tively calm and I recognize them for what they are – a need to just get out the emotions and hopefully feel better afterward. I stood at the bottom of the stairs and listened to see if this cry was one of those, or if it was one that triggers the mom instinct that says – "Run! Your baby needs you." This one quickly turned into the latter.

I ran up the stairs, knocked on the bathroom door and then opened it. I found her sitting on the floor, dripping wet with a towel wrapped around her. The shower was still running. One step back. I didn't say much, I simply made sure she knew I was there. As her sobs got harder, she actually began to gag and moved over the sink....just in case. I held back her hair and encouraged her to "just breathe."

When she had calmed a bit, I was able to find out that this emotional outpouring was due to the text messages of a friend talking about attending a dad/daughter dance. She looked at me with those beautiful, big, brown eyes and begged the answer to the question, "Why can't *my* dad be here for me to go to a dad/daughter dance? Everyone else's is, why isn't mine?" My heart, that had felt a little bit healed just moments before, tore open once again and my tears flowed as I held her, wishing desperately that I had an answer to that question.

It is exactly the question I've asked God several times in several ways since June 18, 2009 when her dad was taken from this earth far too soon. "Why God? Why did you leave this vulnerable, sweet, daddy's girl without her daddy? I think I might be OK.... eventually....with a lot of work and grief processing and writing and venting and tears and time, but why would you put our daughter through this? What exactly are You thinking? It is so hard to be a teenager period, and now you've added this to her life story??!!!"

Eventually she declared, "I just want to go to bed." I went into her room and miraculously found some pajamas for her. (We have an agreement – bedroom dig out once a month. We were only three days post dig out, so I was able to find what she needed). I cleared a spot on her bed, tucked her in and sat with her. I started to talk but she said, "I don't want you to talk mom." So I took her cue and suppressed my natural instinct to try to make everything better with words. How long will it take before I realize that as much as I would love to, I can't explain away her heartache? I let her know I was near if she needed me for any reason.

I hate this! I hate that my 16 year old daughter has this heartache in her life. I hate that she knows such a deep grief at such an early age. I hate he has already missed some of her life milestones: her first "official" date, her getting her license, her first drive herself and a friend to the mall trip, her first experience at getting lost and needing directions home. I hate that at points in her future, she will be reminded over and again that her father is not with her: her high school graduation, her college or career choice, her wedding day, his first granddaughter or grandson, and so many more events that could have been that much sweeter, if shared with the person she loved most in this world.

It is now 11:30pm and very quiet in my house. My dear, sweet, broken-hearted daughter is sleeping as I do what I've done so often lately—vent writing. My prayer is that God would give her sweet dreams tonight, perhaps of a very happy time in her life when her daddy was still with her. But my deepest soul desire is that, with God's help, she will continue to take those three steps forward and make it through a life that has already dealt her some major setbacks; that she will hang on to the promise that someday, in God's timing, she will be reunited with her daddy and if she wants, she will be able to dance with him for an eternity. If I'm very lucky, maybe she'll let me cut in for a few millenniums.

Psalm 56:8

"You have taken account of my wanderings; put my tears in Your bottle."

- odc

Letters

"There is healing when you write."

That is the belief of our speaker in grief support as she talked about the subject of guilt—specifically true guilt (feelings of guilt about a moral failure) false guilt (feelings of guilt without a moral failure) and shame (strong feelings of defectiveness and brokenness about who you are; "I am a bad person"). I listened with great interest to this topic and left that evening so grateful that I wasn't dealing with excessive guilt and shame, in addition to the grief of losing my husband to cancer. And I say that not as a pat on the back to me, but as a pat on the back to him. He was so easy to love and be a life partner to; so willing to forgive my blunders as a person who was "created to be loved perfectly by God, but not loving perfectly."

Oh don't get me wrong, there were times earlier in my grief when I had some guilt messages play with my mind: What if we had never messed with that very first tumor, would the cancer have spread? Did we do everything possible? Did I show/tell him enough that I loved him?

Letters of healing. That was the suggestion to those who were wrestling with guilt and/or shame. I liked that the letters could be written to whomever necessary; God, the loved one, even yourself. And they could also project any emotion necessary; anger, love, gratitude, apology, forgiveness, unsaid words, recalling memories.

I've been writing my thoughts for several months now and totally agree with the belief that writing can be healing. It has definitely played a role in my grief process. So although my writing hasn't been in a letter format, the letter suggestion reminded me of an unexpected gift that Gary left for me that helped me answer one of my guilt questions.

It was the basement remodel plans that set the gift discovery events in motion. In order to transform our 25+ years of marriage storage area into the home theater/man-cave/self designed bathroom of his dreams, we had to do some ***major*** clean out. My husband was a pack rat, and many times I questioned why he wanted to save the various things he saved like: a lone bowling pin, our daughter's baby teeth (yes, I'm serious) boxes of books left in the crawl space of our first house by the original owners that he moved over to the next house we bought, every rug we ever owned, and rings of unmarked keys to who-knows-where locks.

Due to his pack rat tendencies, our clean out process didn't get completed before the scheduled start of construction, so Gary moved a lot of things to his outside shed, with the intention of sorting through it at a later date. But when he got sick so quickly, that shed clean out process fell to me. With the help of my daughter, sister-in-law, niece and nephew, we tackled it.

Because the anti pack rat member of the family (i.e., me) was now making the decisions, the toss pile was pretty big. But during the purge process, we discovered a treasure. It was a box that contained a stack of love letters that I sent to Gary the summer he proposed to me. When I opened the lid and saw the "rare in these days" handwritten envelopes, I immediately flashed back to that summer when the almost nightly cards and letters from the country girl to the city boy were written and mailed. I couldn't believe he had saved them after all these years.

Later, when I went up to our bedroom where he spent the last seven months of his life, he asked for a full report on the clean out process. He wanted to make sure I hadn't thrown out his baseball mitt (of all things!). I assured him I hadn't, and then told him I had found the old love letters. He smiled his quirky smile with the single raised eyebrow which loosely interpreted meant, "oh yeah baby." I climbed up in our big bed next to him that night and as he slept, I silently re-read each letter. I was sweetly reminded of the thrill of early love, and the anticipation I felt to start our lives together so many years ago. Okay, I'll admit it. For once, I'm **glad** Gary had his pack rat tendency.

So back to that one guilt question – Did I show/tell him I loved him enough? My early love letters were just the start of our often vocalized and demonstrated love story that ended far too soon. But now I'm intrigued with the thought of a new question — Can we **ever** show/tell someone we love them enough? I vote no. I still tell him.

Song of Solomon 8: 6 & 7a

"Put me like a seal over your heart, like a seal on your arm, for love is as strong as death, jealousy is as severe as Sheol; its flashes are flashes of fire, the very flame of the LORD. Many waters cannot quench love, nor will rivers overflow it."

- odc

Purpose

What's the point? That's the topic we tackled last night in grief support.

I remember wondering that a lot in high school as I endured some of my required classes. I kept thinking, "Will my 'success' post high school really be impacted that greatly if I can't solve an algebraic equation or memorize the chemical periodic table?" My peers were asking that same question as they struggled through Shakespeare, but since English was "my thing" I never questioned the point of the Bard of Avon.

Most everyone, at some point, poses the What's the point? question on a much grander scale. It is asked as it relates to Life (capital L). And since we gravity bound humans are uncomfortable with unanswered questions, we then try to answer it with earthly things: jobs, money, material possessions, relationships, fulfilled goals, travel, adventure, fun, adrenaline activities, etc. None of these things are bad in and of themselves, but they are all temporal, finite, fleeting, and deep within us is the desire to do or be something that transcends our days on this planet. When the head hits the pillow, too many are haunted with the question – "Is this really all there is to life?"

Rick Warren has written a book called <u>The Purpose Driven Life</u> that proposes the real answer to that question is to live a life that is based on God's eternal purpose and not cultural values. It was a book that affirmed mine and my husband's beliefs, faith and life goals. Together, we had a plan of action and the focus to live out the purposes God was placing before us.

Just when we thought we had it all figured out, What's the point? came roaring back into our lives when my husband was diagnosed with cancer and the answers didn't seem to come at all. I remember thinking—if it's true that *all* things work together for the *good* of those who love God and have been called according to His purpose (Romans 8:28) and we fell into that love God/living His purpose classification, what possible *good* could come from cancer? There was nothing good about surgeries and BCG treatments and chemotherapy and mouth sores and ambulances and blood clots and seeing my handsome, strong, rarely ever sick husband become physically weaker as each day passed.

"There is a reason." Those are the words I heard my husband say several times when he talked with friends and family members about his cancer diagnosis and battle. Once again, a man of few words. There was no lengthy theological explanation, or the reading of long scripture passages, or an extended, rambling dialogue that discussed the spiritual factors as they relate to physical suffering and faith. His answer to the question What's the point? was, "I don't know, but I trust God has a reason." His faith and his four words during this time of turmoil seemed too simplistic to me and didn't answer my behind-closed-doors, clenched fists, tear filled What's the point? and What can You possibly be thinking? questions (shouts) to God. But Gary never wavered from his deeply entrenched faith filled point of view. He might not have been physically strong in the end, but his spiritual strength was as strong as ever, and that is what mattered most.

As I was planning Gary's final "celebration of life" service, I was contemplating the musical selections that would artisti-cally communicate the message of how he lived his life—in a way that answered the What's the point? question so beautifully in God's eyes. It was my daughter that reminded me of a song by Caedmon's Call entitled, "There is a Reason." It was such an obvious choice. It was Gary's mantra. I'm positive he is proud of the fact that she suggested this song so that we could remember his faith statement that very difficult day and in years to come.

So it's nine months now since I said my earthly goodbye to my first love, and there are signs that I am healing enough to face that What's the point? question yet again as it relates to my greatly changed life circumstances. It is my heart's desire to seek out and fulfill whatever role or project God places in front of me that will honor Gary's mantra because I believe, just like he did, that even in the worst earthly circumstances, when we don't understand the purpose or the point, there is a reason.

Isaiah 61:3 (making it personal)

(Lord thank You for Your promise) "To grant those who mourn in Zion, giving them a garland instead of ashes, the oil of gladness instead of mourning, the mantle of praise instead of a spirit of fainting; so they may be called oaks of righteousness, the planting of the Lord, that He may be glorified." (Because that is a purpose worth pursuing).

- odc

Firsts

Part of living is experiencing the "firsts" in life. Some of our "firsts" cause our hearts to warm when we recall them: the first two wheeler bicycle, the first date, the first kiss, the first time we say the words "I love you," the first TRUE love, the first car, the first job, the first paycheck. Then, there are those "firsts" we'd like to have never experienced and still wince a bit as we think of them: the first trip to the emergency room, the first breakup, the first heartache, the first conflict in an important relationship that leaves you angry and hurt.

When my husband Gary died in June of 2009, it was like time got cut in half. I thought I was done with facing many of life's firsts (both good and bad) but his death became like a bright red, extra thick, permanent marker slashing through the horizontal timeline of my life. It marked an event that brought about unwanted endings and would begin a whole new series of firsts.

First holidays without your loved one are hard. The very first for me was Fourth of July. For many years, we had joined Gary's side of the family at his parents' house to celebrate our nation's independence. They lived on the street where the parade passed and within walking distance to the park where all of the festivities took place. We would all gather in, bringing our favorite summer food selections and usually several friends to mix in with the relatives. The kids and teenagers would immediately disappear together into the park for rides and games and fishing. They also had the job to go over to the hill, in front of the pond where the bands would be playing, and stake out the Casten territory with blankets and folding chairs so that later in the day, we could all reunite for the music and the firework display that is one of the best in the Chicago suburbs.

It was just over two weeks after Gary's funeral that the Fourth holiday hit. My daughter asked if we were planning to go this year, and I, wanting to prove that I was "brave" immediately answered, "Of course, we can't break tradition." She was glad. We went, and it ended up being a much harder day than I had suspected. Walking back into his parents' home without him was so hard. He was usually the grill master on the 4th, and I kept looking out to the patio to see if he was there cooking and joking with his nieces and nephews. All day my heart felt like there was a weight hanging from it. When the sun set and it was fireworks time, I chose not to go over to the park, but to stay at the house with his mom. We turned off all the lights, raised the blinds in her front room, and opened the front door to hear the patriotic music that highlights the display. For the first time, I cried as I watched fireworks, as I remembered all the times he and I had watched them together, starting with the very first display when we were dating at Chicago's Buckingham Fountain and lakefront, up to just the year before, surrounded with so many of his family members.

There have been several first holidays without him now: his 50th birthday, Thanksgiving, Christmas, New Year's, Valentine's day, and there are a few more significant dates coming up—four more actually, until I will come to that one year date. But it's not only the holidays that are difficult "firsts." Sometimes it's the little events that hit me harder than even the holidays: the first time I walked without him into the church where we together worshipped and served for so many years, the first time I had to state my marital status as "widow," the first phone call that asked to speak to (pause) Gerhardt (usually pronounced incorrectly) the first time I got brave enough to open his junk drawer (one of many, I might add). Recently, it was walking back into our local jewelry store that he so often patronized.

I made the decision to not put away my wedding ring set, like some widows do, but to wear it on my right hand. That meant it needed to be resized, and I was only going to trust *one* jeweler with that important task—the one who Gary had programmed into his cell phone speed dial numbers. I drove into the lot, gathered my courage, talked to Gary for a few seconds, and then entered the doors that he had walked through so many times in the past. One of the owners of the store (who is also a very dear friend) greeted me and together we talked and fought back tears. When the resizing details had been worked out, my friend asked me to put on my "brave face." She brought out a box and informed me that Gary had picked it out for me and had been paying on it when he got ill, and she had been waiting to give it to me at an appropriate time. I opened the box to find a beautiful gold locket. My brave face (which hadn't been that brave up to this point) didn't last long. How typical of my dear husband to arrange for me to receive yet another token of his love, even after he was no longer here to give it personally; and how appropriate that it is a locket where I can place his picture next to mine, and wear it close to my heart, and then someday pass it on to our daughter.

Heart healing. I can feel it, though at times I still have those heavy heart episodes. The first "firsts" were definitely harder than the more recent "firsts," and hopefully the "firsts" to come will follow that same, *somewhat* easier pattern. Some people choose to forget because the pain of the memories is too difficult; I choose to remember because the joy of the memories is worth it.

Philippians 1: 3 (making it personal)

"I thank my God in all my remembrance of you (Gary)."

-odc

Garden Prayers

It's the Easter season and spring has finally come to the Chicago land area. As a matter of fact, today so accurately reflects the fickle Chicago temperatures. It was 75 degrees and sunny, more like summer than spring. No complaints from this lover of warm weather.

"Now is the winter of our discontent." Originally said in the works of Shakespeare, that statement echoed many times through my thoughts as I endured an even more than usual difficult winter in the Midwest. The sub-zero wind chills, the piles of dirty snow, the flu bugs that drive me into hibernation and deprive me from my normally life-giving social interactions, all of these issues can make the many months of cold, gray skies difficult. Add in grief, uncertainty, and a broken heart, and you'll maybe understand why I wondered at times if I'd even make it through this *extreme* winter of discontent. But true to God's planned seasonal changes in the Midwest, hopefully the winter is done (although I do remember tromping through snow in my new white shoes on Easter Sunday as a little girl…) and flowers are once again blooming, and I am looking forward to celebrating Easter—for it was the undeserving, sacrificial act of Christ's death on the cross that gives me the assurance and peace that my beloved Gary is safe, healed, happy, rewarded.

For many years, I have read the account of Jesus' final days, but I am seeing it in a new light this year. If we are careful to be in a constant learning process, our life situations can grant us new perspectives on familiar information. I am noticing new things about His prayer in the Garden of Gethsemane. It was there, as He was thinking about his impending death, he began to be deeply distressed and troubled. He says, "My soul is overwhelmed with sorrow to the point of death." That phrase hit me to the very core of my being this year. I recognize that deep sorrow sentiment. I have felt that sentiment. I have struggled to move out of that oppressive, stifling emotion that can overtake every fiber of a grieving person's being.

A little later, He says, "Father, everything is possible for you. Take this cup from me." I've prayed that prayer too. Mine was worded more like, "God, everything is possible for you. Heal my husband's body of this cancer. Get us out of this awful life situation. Do You understand all the implications if You don't?" I prayed that prayer so many times, but just like Jesus' request, the cup didn't get taken from my husband.

There is a final part to Jesus' prayer, and this is the part that blows me away, because I didn't want to say it as it related to my husband's situation. "Yet not what I will, but what you will." I remember when the hospice workers came in those last few weeks and it became obvious that Gary was going to need even more care and more medication dosages. I kept asking the question, "How am I going to do this?" The hospice workers thought I was asking for specific instructions on care giving techniques and medication distribution, but in reality, I was struggling to give voice to the more difficult question that I hadn't had the courage to even think about, much less state. The question of, *"If* it comes to this, how am I going to let him go, the only man who I have loved for over 26 years, the man who promised to take care of me during my health issues, the man who I have helped fight this cancer battle for the past five years?"

Looking back now, I *never* gave up hope that God would take the cancer from Gary's body, but at some point, when it was too difficult to see him in such an incapacitated state, I did come to that clenched teeth, broken hearted statement that relinquished my needs and my desires and my heart's cry, for what would be better for Gary, and was ultimately God's will. I could not see the plan, the wisdom in God taking Gary, but I realized that the faith *talk* that I've had all these years had to become the very real faith *walk* for the final days of his life, the difficult days of planning and carrying out his services, every day that has followed since, and every day that is yet to come.

When Jesus got His answer, which basically was, "I'm not going to take away this difficult situation you are about to go through," I find it interesting what he did ***not*** do. He didn't experience a questioning of his faith, or if God (his Father – can you imagine the anguish of the father heart?) loved Him. He didn't fall into a pile of despair or question if God had even heard his prayer in the first place. He got up and faced the very difficult life event that he had to face. And He did it with the faith filled belief that God knows best.

I heard a quote the other day. "If I had God's power, I would change my circumstances. If I had God's wisdom, I wouldn't." It hit me like a ton of bricks because this Easter, if I had the power, I would be celebrating Easter once again with Gary by my side for our Good Friday trip to Lincoln Park Zoo, our amazing church Easter services and his custom made Easter baskets that he planned so specifically for me and our daughter each year. I'll miss all of that.

God's wisdom, not mine. Someday I'll understand. Until then, I'll trust.

- odc

Mourning

"Grief is what those who have experienced a loss think and feel on the inside. Mourning is the outward expression of those feelings."

I've become a Facebook fanatic. I know some people love it, some people hate it, but I have found it a great social outreach tool to help this particular people oriented person stay connected and reconnect with family and friends. It has been a welcome diversion for my never still mind as I focus my thoughts on what is happening in others' lives, and try to keep from sinking too deeply into the negative, fearful thought waves that can overcome me too often when I'm struggling with all the aspects of the death of my husband.

Recently, my brother-in-law posted this thought on Facebook. "Turns out that they're 'mourning doves,' not 'morning doves.' Who knew? Oh, and your mind really wanders when you're running." His post flashed me back to my childhood days. I grew up in rural Sycamore, IL. My dad wasn't a farmer, but our house was surrounded by cornfields and a small forest, and I spent a lot of time outside. One of the sounds that can flash me back to my childhood is the haunting coo of the mourning dove, whose soft drawn out song sounds like a lament. Even as a child, before I had any major life events that could cause me to think this way, I thought the cry of this particular bird was so sad—beautiful, but sad. So when my brother in law pointed out that it was mourning with a "u", it didn't surprise me at all.

Now that Chicago is finally experiencing spring, the mourning doves have come back to the area and I'm sure there is a nest near my front door because I am hearing them and seeing them so often now. Or perhaps, since my heart is still mourning the loss of my husband, I am just more aware of them and their song strikes a resonant chord deep within me.

I still love to be outside, and so now that the sun has started to shine warmly again, as often as possible, I sit on one of our porches: the back porch in the morning, because it faces east, and the front porch in the evening, because it faces west. The heat of the west sun can get pretty intense during the summers and a few years ago, I mentioned to my husband that if there was only a breeze blowing, the heat on the front porch wouldn't be so intense and I could enjoy the evening sunshine a little more. Well, with my husband, merely mentioning an issue or desire became his personal agenda to make things better or right. Within a week, electric to the porch was wired and a beautiful, big, outdoor fan over the table and chair was installed. And in typical male thinking, there is a remote that turns the fan on and off and to different speed levels. He was a remote fanatic!

As I sat down to contemplate all the great points of last night's grief session and write, I decided to focus on the phrase above that defines mourning. And then, an unusual thing happened. A mourning dove flew right up to the window that I face when I write, and landed on the porch fan blade, and sang her song of sorrow as her weight made the fan move slowly in circles. It was if she landed there to join me in my mourning today and her coo put a voice to my inner sadness that still flares as I "lean into the pain of grief" in order to heal.

Because I'm a little farther down the grief road (and probably because the sun is shining) today my mourning is laced with thankfulness to my God, and that dove's Creator, for having survived my loss so far. Because, like others, with the first steps away from his cemetery plot came those unavoidable thoughts that this was my breaking point, the final days of hope and happiness have passed; the pain of this death will be more than I can bear. But just like that mourning dove whose song sounds like the outward expression of a deep loss, I am learning to mourn, to give action to my grief through tears, talking, and writing. And though life seems to be charcoal gray, and the songs of my soul seem to be in minor keys, I am learning there is still beauty that can shine through the monochromatic hues of life without him, and the minor melodies of my forever changed heart song.

Sing on mourning dove. You inspire me to do so too.

- odc

Circumstances

"God is not a circumstantial God."

When I reflect back on the great times in my life, there are several that stand out. A few that come to mind are: the first time I saw the ocean, the night my boyfriend (who later became my husband) said he loved me as we were strolling through Kankakee River State Park, the day he proposed to me sitting on the front porch swing of my country home, our wedding day, the day he carried me over the threshold of our first home, the day we got the phone call that said a young 16 year old girl had picked us as potential parents for her unborn child, and then the day that that baby girl was placed into our arms to parent, the day of her christening—where we dedicated to raise her up in the Christian tradition, the day our daughter made her own public display of Christian faith by being baptized, and so many more that weren't marked by big events, but just by doing life as best as we could, where God had placed us.

It was so easy on those days, and the days surrounding these great events, to be content, calm, and confident in life, and in my faith, and in giving God praise. It was easy to link these descriptors to God's name: loving, caring, faithful, good, easy to trust.

But as with every life, my life has also weathered storms. None of us expect life to be perfect, those fairy tale endings never had many of us fooled, but recently it seems there have been too many of us being confronted with very hard life situations. For me personally, it has been my husband's cancer, his valiant fight, his death, and all the residuals that come with that gaping absence in my life. And it has been trying to help my daughter through her loss, in addition to the issues that come with being a 16 year old. And it has been the decision to try to keep my husband's roofing company going, in spite of the tough economy and the many factors that make keeping a business going difficult. Just like that happy events list, there are many more hard situations that aren't necessarily big events, but just come as a result of doing life.

Admission: my good time God descriptors were challenged. Oh, I never said them out loud, but in my mind they were popping up: distant, uncaring non-existent, unwise.

And yet, the statement above, which was mentioned in my grief support lesson last week, challenges me. Because it tells me what I already knew—that in both the good and bad life circumstances, God doesn't change. He was there loving me and delighting in my reaction when I saw the ocean for the first time, and He was there loving me and knowing the shock and fear I felt when the diagnosis was cancer. He was there to delight in the joy I felt when my greatest desire to be married to my husband became a reality, and He was there feeling my heart break on the day when I had to say good bye to him (for now). It was *my* emotions and state of mind that changed with the circumstances.

God has been there, in *all* circumstances—all knowing, all powerful, never changing. On the days when I felt Him, and on days when I wondered if He cared. On the days of wondering if I could watch my husband sit down in the chemo recliner for yet another treatment, and on the days when I felt His strength to serve my husband and love him into heaven in his final days. And since that day, God has been there in the times when I feel like I won't ever be happy again, and on days when hope comes sweeping into my soul for the days He has planned for my future.

Recently, I woke up in the middle of the night and this phrase came to me—*Because in the end......there is heaven.* I feel like it was a "God whisper" (thank you Bill Hybels) the breakthrough in a rough three week span. I'm not sure if it was because it was the first Easter without my husband, then followed by my first birthday without him in many years, or the fact that I'm starting to see glimpses of what my next "purpose" might be based on my changed life situation and someone wants to derail my usefulness by keeping me in a sorrow filled, bewildered, ineffectual state.... but I spent about three weeks battling negative thoughts, fear, anxiety, physical symptoms and hopelessness. I did everything "text book" style to break the pattern. I prayed, I asked others to pray for and with me, I talked, I journaled, I studied God's word, I tried to divert my mind, I focused on the desperate need of those in global poverty, I ate chocolate and drank mochas (what—that's not textbook?)....nothing seemed to work.

And then, I believe the heaven thought was a gift from the gracious God who is now taking care of my husband *far* better than I ever could. No matter what happens here on earth, my non-circumstantial God has promised heaven. That is not hinging on cash flow, or perfection, or companionship, or bank accounts, or emotions, or the direction of the wind, or the price of tea in China. Peace at last, at least for now. I need to hang on to that thought!

Now *that* is a fairy tale ending.

John 16:33
"These things I have spoken to you, so that in Me you may have peace. In the world you will have tribulation, but take courage, I have overcome the world."

- odc

Chapters

R eading has always been a passion of mine, perhaps because growing up in the cornfields of Sycamore, IL left me with few options for down time activities. I was reading even before kindergarten, and can still remember the excitement of browsing through the books in our elementary school library in order to have something new to read. I may have been in rural IL, but often I would travel far beyond the borders of DeKalb County, to the new places where gifted writers could take me.

I currently have five books sitting on my desk that I'm in the process of reading. That's not unusual. What is unusual is their topics and the way I'm reading them. I'm usually very structured, and so my rule has always been to finish a book before starting a new one. But par for the course these days, grief has thrown off all my "usuals" and has even affected my book reading, so that whole finish regiment is not working so well.

One of the five books was sent to me by one of my husband's dearest friend and mentor. It's called <u>God on Mute</u>. He read it and asked other friends to read it that have had some tough life events and may be feeling like God is not, or didn't respond to their many prayers during that time. (I'm pretty sure I was near the top of his list of friends that might fall into that category). Then there is a book called <u>More Than an Aspirin</u> loaned to me by a friend who falls into my spouse loss friends category. The subtitle is "A Christian perspective on pain and suffering." Notice a pattern on the topics?

Recently, in grief support, our speaker said this statement. "Consider this loss a very sad chapter in a very good book." Oh man....I like that! How many of us, when we're reading a book, stop at the saddest chapter and put the book down? Okay, so I'll admit that there are some books that end sadly and we have no other choice, but that doesn't have to be the case in my life story.

I've been feeling like the grief/loss/mourning fog I've been stumbling through lately is permanent, never-ending, all invasive. I've been stuck in the sad chapter, not able to imagine other options for the remaining chapters. I think part of the reason is because my "everything is going to be OK" guy is no longer around, plus the "everything that can go wrong will go wrong" philosophy seems to kick into high gear when you're grieving, or at least it seems that way.

The loss of a loved one is a *huge* life event that needs to be processed in a very intentional way for a matter of time. The hows and how longs of that last statement are unique to each circumstance. I don't think it is wise, nor God's plan, that grief be stuffed, ignored, rushed through or diverted by some other comfort tactic. On the other hand, the grieving process is exactly that – a process and the darker areas of grief are not where God wants us to stay. And I know for a fact it is not where Gary would want me to stay.

"Turn the page." That's what God seems to whispering to me. My response? "I don't **want** to. Gary and I were forever joined characters with a plan on how we would live out the rest of our story and then You changed the whole plot line by introducing the conflict called cancer into our story. I liked my story and the way it was progressing."

Our story was not a fairy tale. Things weren't perfect because the characters were not perfect (including and especially the **main** character in **my** story—**me**!). Some days, our story would have more appropriately fallen into the dramatic category (there's a teenage girl in the house) or a comedy, or even into the stranger than fiction sci-fi genre. My protagonist, my hero, my imperfect, but pretty darn close to it partner's earthly storyline has ended, and therefore the rest of my story will be forever impacted by that fact. But my story isn't done yet. God still has more chapters to write. He's still developing the main character and may have new settings and plot lines in store for her.

As I get closer to turning the page....reluctantly....slowly.....I again state my trust in the Author. He knew my story before I was even born. He knows the rest of it. And in spite of my very sad recent chapter, He has blessed me with a very good book so far.

- odc

Trust

S tructure. Order. Planning. Goals. Predictability. Control.
I'll admit it. Those are the things that I like, I do, I strive for.
But disease (and cancer in particular) doesn't play by anybody's
rules, and that can cause even more frustration when you're wired
up like me. And if there was such a thing as a list of commonly
heard words related to mourning and grief, those words would
never make it onto the page.

"Wait. Be willing to accept just enough light for the next step."
That was one of the points made in my grief support session.
Waiting. That usually involves patience, letting someone else control the circumstance, silence, dwelling in the dark, unstructured
time, trust, not knowing. How contrary to how I'm wired. But then
I remembered a time in my life when the "not knowing" became a
great adventure.

It was before we became parents, and Gary and I were young
and a little foolish (some would say more than a little) and had the
luxury of spontaneous travel. There was a family reunion planned

in Tennessee. We decided to go, and extend the trip by adding to the itinerary my very favorite place in the United States, The Outer Banks of North Carolina. And best of all, we were going to do the trip on our motorcycle. We knew the date of the reunion and where we would stay the first night after that – with an aunt and uncle who lived in Tennessee, but then it was going to be a grand adventure that would be decided as each day dawned.

Do you know what a challenge it is to pack two weeks of living needs into a motorcycle saddlebag? Stripping away the not necessaries is the only way that leaves room for the necessities. What seems like a have to have can suddenly become a "not enough room item" when compared to the basic needs like rain gear, a tooth brush and a dry pair of socks.

The trip ended up being fantastic—most of the time. We experienced every kind of weather – heat, rain, fog, humidity. We drove through the beautiful Smoky Mountains, almost got affixiated by exhaust fumes due to sitting in a traffic jam in the Chesapeake Bay tunnel in Virginia; we missed the every four hour ferry out to the Banks by seconds, and ate not by the clock, but by whenever we felt hungry. Late night gas station hot dogs sitting on the curbside never tasted so good.

The first night on Ocracoke Island, my husband commented on how nice it was that our little inn had candles by the bedside. I explained they weren't for ambiance, but because we were sitting right smack in the middle of Hurricane Alley, and if electric went out, candles would be a good backup. That night, a wicked storm rolled in and I remember waking up to see him standing at the window with a look of panic on his face at the thought of his beloved motorcycle getting blown out to sea by the gale force winds that were threatening to do just that.

The return trip from an adventure is never as fun as starting it and that was especially the case when our play it by ear journey was drawing to an end. As we began the long trek home, we ran into a massive heat wave. Being the conscientious motorcyclists that we were, we never rode without long sleeves, jeans, boots and helmets. When you add over 100 degree heat and humidity to that safety attire commitment....well, you get the picture. We stopped at a gas station to fill up after seven straight hours of driving. As I slid off the seat and tried to force my atrophied muscles to support my weight, I peeled off my helmet and feigned that the fact that my hair was plastered to my head was OK with me. Helmet hair is so attractive! In the gas bay next to us sat a highly coiffed lady in her air conditioned luxury car and she looked at us like we were crazy. We both laughed and I said, "Whose idea was this trip anyway?"

So now I'm in this grief journey. Nothing feels structured or ordered. Planning seems stalled. Life is unpredictable and I'm living in the land of not knowing. I'm in that wait mode. My life partner, that made me brave to do unorthodox things, is no longer by my side and there are times when I want to get right in God's face and say, "Whose idea was this trip anyway?"

Trust. That's what it took for me to climb on the back of that motorcycle with Gary and take our over three thousand mile unplanned trip. And trust is what it takes for this wait time. Trust that God has a plan, when mine have all been derailed. Trust that although this loss forced a change on me I did not choose, there can be new lessons to learn, new life skills to develop, new roads to choose and sights to be seen. I'm learning that I don't have to have complete knowledge of what's ahead of me. I need to be open to what an uncharted journey can bring.

I'm packing light and hanging on.

Psalm 25:4

"Make me know Your ways, O Lord; teach me your paths. Lead me in Your truth and teach me, for you are the God of my salvation; for You I wait all the day."

- odc

One Year

Here it comes. A summer thunderstorm is about to begin. I opened the front door of my home this morning to be blasted with hot, humid air so thick that I opted to close the door again—quickly. The sky was overcast and I heard the low rumblings of thunder. It really does sound like the angels bowling, which someone told me when I was a little girl. I could tell at any moment, the heavens would open and rain would pour down.

Here it comes. The one year mark of my husband's death is near. I can't help but relive what was happening in my life one year ago this week. It was a storm of humongous proportions. The clouds of confusion were rolling in as it started to dawn on me that he was slipping away. He talked about going home and we weren't sure if the meds were making him think he was still in the hospital and not at home where he wanted to be, or if he was talking about Home, (with a capital H), where his earthly father, father-in-law, and Heavenly Father were waiting.

In some respects, it seems like June 18, 2009 was many years ago. It seems that way when I think of the lonely hours without him, the length of holidays without him when I just wanted the day to be over, the hours spent doing paperwork related to his death and our business, the sleepless nights and restless days. In some respects, it seems like June 18, 2009 was just a moment ago, and I still can't believe he's not just away for a work week at Camp Paradise and will be rolling in any minute, more than ready for a hot shower where the water doesn't come from a bucket, and time with his girls.

When we were told that the chemotherapy hadn't worked and there was nothing more the medical world could do to help us battle the cancer, Gary's decision was that if he was going to leave this world, he wanted it to be during warm weather because my health condition makes it difficult to be out in cold weather, and it seems like all of our family funerals tend to take place in the bitter months of winter's blast. He told me that. I was amazed, but not surprised, that this was one of his final wishes because even in this circumstance, he was thinking of me first.

When we were planning Gary's celebration of life service, my brother-in-law who is a pastor (or, as I like to put it, our family marry-er and bury-er) asked if my daughter and I would like to say something at the service. I was torn. I am a woman of words, but for some reason I felt like I shouldn't add that task to that day that was already going to be so difficult. I know I would have spent endless hours trying to get just the right thing written. I extended the option to our daughter and she declined, but had a great alternative idea. She decided she wanted to write a letter to her dad, and then send it up to heaven via a helium filled balloon at the grave side. I thought that was a great idea and she graciously allowed me to join her in writing my own final letter to the man who meant so much to both of us.

The day of Gary's service arrived and I felt an unusual peace that day. I was able to focus on Gary's state of being—no pain, no cancer, no chemotherapy or worries about open roofs and unexpected rain storms in Chicago, and not my gaping life loss or many challenges ahead. I felt power and strength beyond my own that I can only credit to Gary himself and God Himself.

As it turned out, that day was a record-breaking heat day in the Chicago area. I had to laugh as I looked up to heaven and said, "Hey babe, I think you over did the heat wish just a bit today." The minute the two red, heart shaped balloons hit the heat; they deflated and didn't have the power to lift the weight of our letters off the ground. It was a moment of laughter for everyone at the grave site, including myself and my daughter. I promised Gary that Chandler and I would be back to release our letters on a cooler day. I tucked them away for safe keeping.

I found our letters this week and my daughter and I decided this one year anniversary week was the perfect time to reattempt our promised launch. I thought that I might want to re-write mine since it was written just days after I had said good bye to him, but the wording was still perfect. My daughter didn't change hers either. We went to his grave site. It is in one of the most beautiful cemeteries I have ever been to. Rolling green hills and sparkling ponds with fountains that fill the air with the sound of water are such a peaceful backdrop for the hundreds of flower filled vases that dot the landscape. Seldom do I visit when I don't see families of deer browsing within the quiet, solemn, reverent, resting place for cherished loved ones. We were armed with a bright bouquet of flowers picked out by my daughter for his vase, two fresh, red, heart shaped balloons with extra long strings, and our letters.

We sat down on the ground by his marker and worked on getting our letters tied tightly. When that was done, we looked at each other and cried. It was so hard to think about letting the balloons go, but then my daughter said these words to me, "Mom, wouldn't it be cool if someday, when we meet Dad in heaven, he is holding our letters?" Although the tears flowed even more, we smiled at that awesome thought. We finally got up the nerve to let go of the strings, and the balloons slowly rose, riding the wind currents higher and higher and up over the tree line until we could not see them anymore.

Today is June 18, 2010. One year. It's another hot, humid day in the Chicago area. Right now it is sunny, but the forecast is for thunderstorms tonight. Let them come. I have faced tough life storms and the Calmer of the Storms has empowered me to cry, to question, to remember, to grieve, to laugh, to grow, to trust, to survive, to think about thriving again. God has a plan. I believe that He can use even this loss to shape me into the person He wants me to be to fulfill that plan. I will honor Gary and his memory forever by seeking out that plan, and fulfilling it to the best of my God given strength and ability.

Thinking of you, on your one year promotion date my love.

- odc

ODC

At the end of each of my writings are the letters ODC. They stand for *one day closer.*

The days since my husband slipped from reality to eternity have been the hardest I have ever had to live, so far. His death elicits great sorrow and joy within the same heartbeat. We knew and experienced and cultivated a deep love, and my grief over his death has been every bit as deep and intense. I had a friend tell me that if he had the choice of bypassing the pain by erasing the memories, he would never do it. And even though on days I think the loss is more than I can bear, he bet that I would never give up my memories of Gary for the sake of forgoing the pain. He was spot on!

In spite of my wishes for life to not ever be this way—it is. That's a cold, hard fact, and at times it makes me want to revert back to a childlike temper tantrum where I kick and scream and throw myself on the floor and cry and then pout for a week. If you have had a loss this deep, you aren't surprised at all by that confession. Maybe you wouldn't go the child temper tantrum route. Maybe you're more the break something type of person, or the one who has become sarcastic and bitter, or the one who feeds the hurt in some way through food or drink or drugs or shopping. Or maybe you're the one who stays overly busy and committed to events and tasks and people, in hope that the constant ache in your heart will be dulled by a never ending to do list.

I'm convinced the source of all evil would love for those of us in the throes of grief to stay in the paralyzing, painful, early stages of grief. I call it the dark stage of grief. It's a place of hopelessness and sadness and ineffectiveness and anxiety and it doesn't make one iota of a difference if you are an atheist, an agnostic, a brand new Christian or one who has lived a life to honor God for many years. The darkness spares no one.

And so we great lovers of the lost move forward into life. Forever changed. Forever catching our breath when we experience the triggers, forever familiar with the tears that burn our eyes and the dull ache that we feel deep within, at random and unexpected times. We don't want to, but we are left with no option than to navigate the changes this loss has caused.

As I turn out the lights each night and head upstairs to bed, these words echo through my soul — *one day closer*. The day has ended. God in His mercy and graciousness has helped me make it through another day without my husband, another day of rediscovering who I am (without him) and what God wants me to accomplish in this new, unexpected life situation. I am one day closer to my own exit from this world and a reunion with the God who has carried me through this storm of grief. One day closer to be reunited with Gary and other loved ones who were welcomed Home before me. That thought carries me.

I hope this book has given you a new sense of hope to move forward into the lighter shades of grief gray—one day at a time. But more importantly, I pray that you are inspired to run toward God in your grief, not away from Him, because He longs to draw near to the broken hearted. He longs to bring hope to your heart. And today, we are all one day closer.

Acknowledgements

This book would never have become a reality without the encouragement from many family members and friends who convinced me that my loss, and the lessons I learned from it, could possibly help others going through their own loss. Thank you for your words that somehow sank in through the thick fog of grief.

I owe an immeasurable depth of gratitude to the leaders, speakers, musicians and volunteers at the Willow Creek Grief Support Ministry in South Barrington, Illinois. This ministry played a key role in helping me start the grief journey. As we gathered together on Monday evenings, we listened and learned and shared. We cried and laughed and felt the occasional breeze of hope from God's comforting truths. We were a "community of sorrow." My heart broke with my own pain, and I experienced a deeper compassion for those who knew that very same pain due to their own spouse's death. It was in these intense times of shared brokenness that the seed of healing was planted in my soul.

The pictures in this book were taken by the following individuals. For the use of their talented photographs, I am forever grateful.

Foggy Road, page 21 – Julie D. Ross (my dear sister)
Tunnel of Love, page 30 – Aaron Mayes
Camp Paradise Riverfront, page 47 – Curtis Vanden Bos
Coffee Message, page 52 – Susan Listhartke
Author Picture – Emily Hernandez photography

And finally, but most importantly, all praise goes to my God who is my Comforter and is in the process of healing me, giving me new direction, new strength, new hope. He has truly blessed and kept me, lifted his countenance upon me and given me peace. He has made His face to shine upon me, and has been ever so gracious to me.

CPSIA information can be obtained at www.ICGtesting.com

235263LV00001B/8/P

9 781613 795521